Tourist To Ecstasy

Tourist To Ecstasy

Tim Lilburn

Toronto / Exile Editions / 1989

This edition is published by Exile Editions Ltd.
69 Sullivan Street, Toronto, Ontario, Canada M5T 1C2

SALES DISTRIBUTION
GENERAL PUBLISHING CO. LTD.
30 LESMILL ROAD, DON MILLS, ONTARIO M3B 2T6

Typeset in Times Roman by Tumax Typesetting Company Limited
Designed by Harold Kurschenska

ISBN 0-920428-29-0

The publisher wishes to acknowledge the assistance towards
publication of the Canada Council and the
Ontario Arts Council.

COVER ILLUSTRATION
Finnbar Strife after an
engraving by William Blake

Contents

Acknowledgements

Some of these poems have appeared in Writing, Quarry, The New Quarterly, Descant, Exile and in the anthology *Christian Poetry in Canada*. "Call To Worship In A Mass For The Life Of The World" and "Elohim Mocks His Images For The Life Of The World" were part of a liturgical drama, co-authored with Maggie Helwig, first performed at St. Jerome's College, Waterloo.

I wish to thank Canada Council and the Ontario Arts Council for their financial assistance.

for Dosia Junor, fierce, doting,
IN MEMORIAM

Ways of Light

---

1. Fervourino To A Barn Of Milking Doe Goats Early Easter Morning

Maāpe, maāpe, maāpe, hust, hust, boobies, dears,
I want to speak to you.   I will turkey Gospel to you
                                        as John Diefenbaker spoke French.
Glitter unto me on your pert, bone-seamed, Rockette legs,
Blue udders whopping knee scoops, snappy
            at the starlet canter of Flesh in a breathless, wartime dress.
Our text: *Ubi caritas et amor.*
Which is that today the Lord High Being of Milk squirted
Life-like from the squeeze of his will. Pseudo-reindeer, attend.

And I say to you
Look at the light on the blond wheat straw.
Energeiai of the Godhead, first seen by Simeon the New Theologian, 1000 AD,
Mt. Athos, now here, cherub bum bright, curves warm from bedding.

To what shall the Kingdom of Heaven be compared?
I say it shall be like the femininity of long grass
Where the New Idea spreader
Arced greenly yesterday's scrapings of the barn floor, vague,
Nevertheless, as the violet of the buck's penis.
And still it shall be like the goat that's stolen the poem
From under the herdsman's pencil, up, suddenly, on the jokes
Of its Pan legs, poem in its pink teeth, then, ears back, off
                                        like a Mozart flute.

Think of the bucks.
Koranic dogmatists, mystically dense as fashion models,
Who clench their bodies in memory always,
            blinking at the flesh exclamatory donging their knees, naming God.
They neither labour nor spin
Yet the Yahweh of Armies jolts them tall with fresh male dreams
While inches of assent bud yearly to their taffied, yellow horns.

Petites, consider not the world.
There the lust-a-rama of the shopping malls humiliates eros,
                                        then naps apodictically, Amen.
Listen, I go now to the kid barn
To preach there to the applause of their lips
Five streams of milk
From the black nippled lamb bar.

And there wads of their coats shall stand up as Dostoevsky at insight
And their ears fall back as a long woman fainting into love,
And they shall know me there, I
Who tickle hail to their beating skunk tails,
As mother,
Which, Isaiah 62: 4-5,
I am, God's wife.

2. Pentecostal Exhortation To A Goat Barn Before First Milking

– for Pat and Ramelle

The barn floats
over its stone foundations
weightless with arousal

above your milk flowers.
Bach organ
shadows in the recital hall rustle and cough
of the 5:00 am, eating barn
roam under one electric light;
milk sings down your udders,
its unhearable white voice,
milk's bright ghost brooding down upon the farm.
Stick-slapping the wooden feeders with canes
we boil you into the parlour.
The farm rises and sways
and walks its hill to morning.

Blank out death, fools of Christ.
When the beaters of the rusted-through spreader
hit a cement chunk, lifted from the barn floor,
on the money, the parabolic wow
the stone describes
out through the shit wash spray
is joy.
This urge
to inhale self
into a white lake in you
what is it
but desire for heaven?

The Green Lobe of God's Brain, Country From St. John's Sideroad North to Lake Simcoe

"External Nature, too, is divine,
mind slumbering in externality."
G.W.F. HEGEL, *Philosophy of Mind*
for L.M.

Everything "dead" trembles
north of the apple-breathed horses and the Dominican cows, rocking
– O sweet Jesus –
slain by sleep, in their choir of hide-polished hazels
at Strawbridge Farm.
The under-earth from Keswick to Pefferlaw lights up with root flame,
Bolts, miles long, white, of vegetable lightning.
Here is the see of heron, bishop, diocese, here, of his living bone,
Parishionered by the barns, widow-plain and pious,
Doukhobor-women-fat and their daycare
of the blond, shirt-tailed corn
In its tag-playing melees, and by the haremed, churchwarden,
Tory bulls, spoken to by clover-fogged dreams
at dust roll;
North, pasture turning biblically to salt,
Sloughs meatier and milky as an old dog's eye near the lake,
creeks, trees growing
Out of water, the last fence line shrugging,
then walking under the coppery wash, everything "dead" trembles.
Corn-rowed clouds by day and by night, clouds
grapey as the curls of a too sensuous god, ecclesial podunkdom here
of bonebird.

A black man, nightly, here, at the Savannah Hotel, in a petroleum tux, sings
Lux above his trancey Georgia organ *O bring back that lovin' feelin'*
O O O that mm-mm feelin'
As deer salmon-arc through maple lots,
their bum-stutter white as the soft dashlights of necking teenagers on milk-
blue roads near Bradford,
While beered-up potato pickers, in the wave-kissed hotel itself, workbooting
a yahoo, liturgical shuffle, their golden, froth-pumpkined
heads making them like Giotto saints, rise – *O O O O* –
Baseball caps first, now, through the hotel ceiling of cobweb and pine.

That feeling which is of hookah dreams
of the concubined bulls which comb the pastured Friesians smooth,
and of the blue towns, hereabouts, and of the green whirring cloud
over mill ponds,
the land's clear mind gathered from the white deer
copulating – flash-dot-flash – a holy Morse among aspens,
the Quaker quiet towns, the perfect apophatic fields,
and consciousness, gold, in vast purple afternoons,
within apples, Ida Reds, fallen
in hair of Hackett's orchard grass.
The earth's mind in its ghostly sleep.

At wood middle, heron, half a woman, council of one,
Raises his head of smoke.
He is gyno-glyph of the hysterical earth, word like the ideogrammatic
body
Of the one horse kept by the rich salesman at Hilltop Farm.
He is peace word, longlegged cypher of the hidden
Female world, and scribbles himself shakily across air.
He mounts in splendour vested to his pulpit in the dead elm.

That feeling which is the feeling nothing
dies. Nothing. Stouffville-ward,
a farmer feels the wobbly, white tongue
of the to-be-born in the Hereford's leafy womb,
calf's tongue white because it is the blind edge of the unseen
world sucking tit-wild at his fingertips – *aah, aah,*
say the farmer's hands.
He thinks, calf lined up, hooves in the prayer position
of birth, his arm gone to the shoulder within the earth-blue bag,
of his wife making coffee up above.
That lovin' feelin' gospels the black
psychogogue, the Savannah's singer, the hardly-ever bird's vicar, one last time,
through the snoring hotel.

Nothing dies.
And engines restart on the love roads; and in the wild raspberry
near the Jewish health spa by the rickety lake, one absent-minded Oldsmobile
waits for the Resurrection.
Nothing dies.
Even the man-screaming-out-of-his-skin look of Rocket Richard
mongoosing across the Maple Leaf blueline on February 26, 1957,
thought lost forever, the look, perhaps a wholly new being,
obliquely cross-referenced in St. Dionysius' *Divine Names*,
has not died, but lives, here,
lives still in the brain of the deer who stops among aspens
and looks.
And interiored in stone, here in this place, is a dark magisterium.
And the awe of the first, now dead, cosmonauts here re-assembles
in the small facial bones of the hen-seeing, in dawn
light, fox.

The black man sings *O Oho-oommm*, away from the sleeping hotel, walking to his car
a small suitcase of groans.
And somewhere, deep behind his ear, a subdivision house cat
At a-ha leap lets out a soprano thrill
That shivers long in the damp air. *Silentium, silentium*
in the green cloud of God's brain.

In owl-dom, in Hegel's mental sleep,
streams bellied like dancers, sleep-charismed cows vanishing
in ground cloud, at the bend of the theotokal root,
and in the joy of the white spiders singing, potbellied,
in the beams of the Savannah Hotel, even
The young men fighting in front of the Bradford Arms, the one
Lifting his toe into the crotch of the other,
The one tilting his forehead with almost adoration
Into the collarbone V of the other
Are together, lovers of sorts, in their eerie hallucination
of a womanless night.

Summer, 1963

The doors are open.
"Great Movies" flickers on the t.v.
Hegel has been dead a hundred and thirty-three years.
Night pings, a cooling engine, with crickets, visionary dogs.
The screens are latched.
A boy fondles a 34-D ball of popcorn into his palm.
Atheletic gardens explode from earth in quickly strangled sprints.
The television flutters and chops with the life jerks of a primitive animal
in the womb.
The boy is watching. He has not yet been seduced by a tree.
His scotoma is immense and leathery where stones press out their love to him.
World stuff pushes in at the drapes. It is a darkness and a longing but not
judgement
The world is dead and alive.
Sprinklers searchlight the neighbourhoods.
The world is in its dioestrum days.
Buffalo herd smell still hangs in its thousands in the cottonwood's night shadow,
while the mouth of the t.v. bunts the face watching it, as a breast.

Overhead, Sputnik cups an instrument-blue silence, a mirror, and floats.
It is television's first days.
Tara's Theme lifts from the glowing box, from cave mouth, and the boy goes up
inside it,
the music violiny, peaky, streamlined and happy with fins as flying saucers
appeared in comic books in the late 1950s.
Up he goes, kidnapped, g's occluding his blood thick-black with hypnogenesis. These
are world-lust, ousia-wonder.
He touches his body and rises further with the music. Over Regina, its cosmorama, lights
an anatomical map of angels' gold bloodways, the boy meets the numinous people
of *his* blood – the hero-shine beings (the lawyer, the politician)
he will later be and speaks there with them, hero-high over his city
in the violins' soft, rising, intellectual machine.
The garden runs up to the fire circle edge, the boy's brain-lip, and halts.
A mosquito, blood zeppelin, stumbles in the lampshade.
At Duck's farm, a dog's hearing over emotion, above violins,
field stones slave-sing a heavy tongue. Invisibly.
The boy does not hear them, but hears
the violins fall on the t.v. with exactly the sound of a bra being removed in the backseat
of a Ford the next sideroad over from Duck's.
He gets up and leaves the room.

He returns with a drink and a bag of Hostess chips.   This is the dialectic at work.
The chesterfield, with a regimental love, grips him.   *It's A Long Way To Tipperary.*
He is well; a bus shakes by outside
                    with history's incandescent heaviness.
He will get better.   The night is bloodwarm.
He will become a tourist to ecstasy.
Let it rain.   Let it rain.   Let it rain.
Half-divine itself, the television, corral of ghosts, cave wall
                              drawn on by the dead, their hunt dreams,
feels out for his reassuring face.
The lad's blood rolls the word "hello" on its simple collie tongue.
                              Hefting the tool's newness.   *Hello.*
                                        Hello.
So subjectivity grows in the child,
    grows a fruit to his flesh, "the blossoming forth of nature itself."
Now the spiral and fecund rest of the divinity
            shuffles its pointy black shoes through the neighbourhood –
                              circles the block, mental toecaps clacking.
Now an eagle bends round and round in the boy's sensuality, his warrior intellect.
His subjectivity is the flesh's eagle feather.
Now heavily pectoralled cars, Platonic *logoi*, flex in the streets and take away the girls.
The world is warm; it is night; it is green; it is breathing.
The medicine energy bundle once, a hundred years ago, between the male buffalo's horns now
        unexpectedly erupts, becomes the screen's power source as Lucille Ball's face
            ghosts out like the fizz in his Cream Soda; it is the first days of television
beneath Sputnik's black airbubble.
The lawns sigh pudgily, safe money.   The tree's eros is crucified.
The cat's dreams transliterate *The Ego And Its Own.*

At the Center, A Woman

Singing.
Vines delta from her mouth.
The heavily breasted Christ in the great sleeps of his lactation.
Her voice grows as love arc of the mounting bull,
    stumbling from gravity's coma to take cow between forehooves.
Her voice touches the world, nose to haunch;
The world slopes backward toward it.
Stones sing with her.
The world's spine is the voice, stones near it.
Red woman, red woman, red woman throb-voicing in stones' high choirs.
Stones.
Throat-thrower woman in the whale-bleat, planet-path tenors of orbiting stones.
Yes.
Around here kneecap-tattooing amnesiac tits, stones like baby-ish adult males
    tango and coo.

Her voice is black water under wheat's erect earth.
Uh. Uh.
Her teeth are armies. *Uh.*
Her throat's flex, tree, flowing mass. Cottonwood, beech.
She sings the forest. Energy mezzos.
Mmho Mmho Mmho Ho Ho Ho Ho
Horse, the great woman she holds the horse, the good, neck muscles of the turning horse.
She holds thigh bone, wing, herb, the stare of heron; her spine is smoke,
    bones braided grass.
Hooo Hooo
What she says, what she says, what
She says is the quack of a palm
Cupped under a squeezed armpit.
Wa-hoo, wa.
Wa. Wa.
Hoo.

Learn To Be At Home In This Darkness

– *The Cloud of Unknowing*

The Permanently Drunk Brag This Is Speech

I

Uncle Jack, there.
It is a Darkness in the mouth of the woman who stands on her deck three hours
after supper on Wild Plum Drive,
The shadow of the name she calls. And calls.
A boy, two blocks away, wrestling handlebars as a hunter the antlers
of a wapiti pulls
the front tire of his bicycle down, listening.
Over the water-cloud *sssh* of oscillators, dogs crying among whirled white legs,
the ice cream truck bending into the last street,
He sniffs the meaty black wind which lumbers after his name
And is sad as if a stranger suddenly had touched him on his hip.
Living Dark, Ghost-of-her-mouth,
The shadow of the boy's unreal, shout-bright name
Eats through his forehead, laying oil-coloured eggs in the puffs
beneath his eyes.
From these, now, an intimate absence will grow in him.
* * *
Further, Uncle, glyphs and portents.
Camaros thunder their turns at the one A&W-ed strip-end,
Scrimmaging round the Omega-shaped driveway curve, engines
tantruming, shocks a-jitter as an adolescent knee.
The cars dream of straightaways into bridge abutments, they dream the red
moment, needles giddy, feet sucked gloriously through the floor,
they crazy-leg, in open field, into end zone's hero leap of flame.
Now, still, their transmissions snarl and ping, heavy with earth; now their
Doberman-grin grills slash at the bumpers before, as the late summer
Maroon prairie sky swells with blood-purple, horse-shaped clouds, crowding
as a premonition of orgasm in sleep.
Perhaps something will happen – my back teeth thrum.

Yes, it will happen, for the spine sings warning.
Uncle Jack, the Darkness
is everywhere, Deuteronomic, complete, growing
like grape clusters on limbs of absence, jarring into matter
on tips of cut fingers.

Buffalo grass cleaves with the jaw of an intruder,
sharking toward the wagon circle,
Moon on his bone point.

Look. Carpeted by the living strings of CHAY Midland Sinatraed
into Valhallah Acres,
A bruise-lilac not-thereness snakes on its belly like a Cree hunter,
hidden by the glittering pelt of its prey,
Down upon the bright herd of houses watering by the gold pool beneath
the street lamp,
A rose-black-past-bloom-height-bloozy muscularity – matinee silhouette hissy
with kiss – of nothing.

See it, Uncle Jack? A flesh-hungry darkness
bends like a park of pigeons, on impulse,
round the colourless pivot of common will.
Dark bird, Uncle, I know it, binary blind spot in flesh of the Unknowable Cloud,
Shade's loquacity, dark pillow-talk of the bald, dry hill.
Men gloomed by the clasp of its wing apologize,
leave everything, entering traffic, fading
into speed's mock transcendence.
Zen Fat Man, you must have seen it

Darkness, intelligent, big-stomached bed of bowing light, light the bent
Ever-herding of shine bits, writhing bed and thigh-bank of the shapeless
gold flow, also everywhere,
labouring it to the forms it has.

Uncle, a trouble's now arguing Richter-pitch in my talking bone up to eye-cup,
Shadow-birth, trouble black as wingbone before the stunning hit.
A sentient tooth in my clotted head storms through the skin.
I am bitten, Uncle, by our single blood.

II

Vocatus atque non vocatus, deus aderit.

So.
"You can look at it with the p-eye; you can look at it with the q-eye,
But if you want to open both eyes at once,
You'll go mad," said Wolfgang Pauli.

Uncle Jack, the V-ed shadow down the front of mother's gaping dress,
swims in my fever-blur, leering, lipped
cloth and bone, ogling with gold-shot
widening teeth.
It never gives up the old target of a face, Jack.
Thus difficulties ever Jonah me.
Night's aggiornamento. Camaros churn
At the other A&W-ed strip-end forty-five minutes later.
Beasts-in-their-minds, they break and gas into the End Time, when they will
be lion-flesh,
hoofed with the Omega-shape, Uncle, and terrible jaws.
They are Platonists, cousin, matter's Onans, and twitch
to be fire, heads of flame, lolling on tails of fire.

Perhaps something will happen. Perhaps, on sidestreets,
mangered in the oscillator's triumph arch, the oscillator's royal wave, the Parousia
Will devil up in a gust of Disneyed star sparkle. Sleep now
let us sleep, between our grinding teeth,
Sleep a morsel of each wound in a heaven of gears.
Then wake. Wake; perhaps all will wake well
and be always well; perhaps, then, at last, the masked, father-face dream
will heel without the night light's chalk ring, and will not and no longer
rise over each, his smiling hand
bright with blade, fierce-bright
as the stare of a demented Abraham.

Cedarwood Crescent, Camelot Mews, Orchid Petal Street,
iambic feet that tiptoe to a Tinkerbell, to a metaphorical sleep.

III

Here, here is the cognitive Vinland of This-Is-As-Good-As-It-Gets,
here, one street of glittering cars, a few smoky lights, snug
In a hamburger scented cloud that natters greasily with explosions of litotic
Neon where lttrs are missing like teeth. Welcome.
Women are calling their sons home.
Let them come home, the little ones, pretties, to this village of the brain,
pinch-white in moonlight as Herod's rage face; let them be citizened here,
Here, where metal-in-heat dances on the boulevards to mate and blue
bug-zappers crackle over the flesh-burnt gardens.
"Do not be afraid. Forget fear: lie down, hands at your sides like small
sighs
Think out your prayers into the quivering ear of the totally white Father,
The marble-glinty One floodlit with famished awareness."
Some have married the cloud risen in their flesh. They are mounting to nothing.

Right now, asleep or wide-eyed over his dangerously raced engine, who does not
feel his blood
Adam's appled up and down in his well-pruned head
By the continuous swallowing of the next-door and for-miles-ever-after Night?
Fingernail now to the depth-sucked shore – beyond the Atlantic of All-fear,
Of which our lives are the wavy, brittle, gold-leaf shadow
flung by its acrobating mass, we, a backward
Crafty people tribal scarred with the salesman leer of Mr. Happy Face,
Old Yellow Head, the God,
Tuning our carburetors for journeys we cannot imagine.

Our ancestors wore horn. This was hardened will and
between their caps of airborne bone, stars
Teased them beyond the sheer drops of their eyes.
We have become a backwater colony of heaven, inbred, malarial.
The Dark fjords into the shore stone of our consciousness
in jags of scary weeping,
In delphic tremors shocking the idle hand that erupts from the shaking wheel.
The permanently drunk brag this is speech.
But here in the State of Blank,
north of Give-Up, compassed by the upturned hand, the shoulder
Peaked then dropped, we are visited seldom, actually, by angels, the ancient,

famous Sky-lords, operatic, touchy, fictioned in the papyri
of the Old Religion
to envy us; seldom do they come among us, slumming, aristocrats at a yard sale,
kicking through the twelve slice, cardboard pizza boxes
stacked and decomposing on our lawns.
* * *
They, however, hallelujah, comet-rare, chaotic as infatuation, they do, they
rave to hunt us. Then
Like electron blurs, there-not-there, we see them without warning through
the pill-sheen lamination of our eyes
Cut hands over locked bone sockets,
the tight jaw muscle of the insomniac,
over the Jansenist neck of the one whose blood-drained grip
on herself is the strangler's,
Geigering, the breathless hands, marvellous hands, witching the one-in-a-million
speechlessly beautiful pain disc.
Rough teeth-tested coin stamped with our own cry-mouthed image
Which they in their monstrous intelligence cannot manufacture,
which we hold no longer as tender.
They wear them as ornament like sun-tips of eagle feathers, like incisor teeth
in a necklace, tendon threaded
to make muscular and splendid the termagant awe of themselves.
Occasionally, in shameless daylight, the eye grogging from nod, they will turn
on a man,
Anyone under a grey hat in a crowd, and pop out his hip.
That man after is useless.
His eyes are hurricanes.

Uncle Jack, you who retired at fifty, shaved your armpits, squeezed my knee
with a giggle everytime my jaw slacked and my eye
went to Paris, you who badgered Jehovah Witnesses on your doorstep
in the afternoons for cash, you perhaps holy fool, did you see them?
the Dark Ones, Rilke's Beings,
feathered at the bases of their skulls with the long, black
absences between electrons,
Through whose several eyes the next life can be dully seen
Scintillating like a field of June corn in blue-edged noon light,
a field and a hill?

IV

These are their holy names – Wanting To Cut Your Wrists, Never to Sleep,
Shame To The End and Sudden Love.
They are mentioned in the old books under amazing aliases.
They have the religious appetite of God's superannuated whales.
Serendipitous hunger pulls them, torn air shrieking, from mythy sky-tip,
down upon the dull republic of the heart's flat line; they home
Upon the cloud man who knows himself
married to the engine of a violent absence, a want-past-want that ghosts him
shakily.

Eat us, dark persons of air and loss; O eat us new.
The frightening-lucky in their magenta fear-bellies, self-laboured, squirm
To be born once more.

V

Most awful, Old Dream, childhood's Noumenon,
Ancient Mariner of the Nerve Lanes, freezes me
With his panic eye, fists bunched, lifting me by my bone lapels.
Remember, remember, sour breathed he breathes,
The medicine wheel, the perfect Egyptian circles
Of sky. Think again of the possible-impossible
Intimacy of heaven, the oval of it, spirit plumpness, shell-rinded,
White in mind. This is the Kingdom-wish, the Idea
Of you in the hands of female trees,
The meta-sexual stones, in your mother's hands,
Father's, in the hands of the woman at the bus stop
At Broadview and Queen; this is the dream of the love-ring,
the flesh-matter

Splice, fat with the yodel of glistening haecceity, the wind-
In-the-brain-strings hum; this the
Blood-rosed, stomach-softening, love-warm song of being.
It is one with the Zeitgeist radared faintly
On the car radio; it is drummed by the vein
Jumping in the belly of the pregnant mare grazing
North of town that beats-out in sympathy
The ejaculation of quanta in the still star
In Galaxy X.
Remember.
The Old Dream still, mother of desire.

* * *

My life turns in an arabesque of decorous consent.
"Go with this nothing, moved only by your love of God.
For myself, I prefer to be lost in this nowhere,
Wrestling with this blind nothingness,"
Said someone whose name was its shadow, whose book is somewhere
in the condominiums, lost on the sun side of the water, an unsaying
of the poly-jointed Nous tongue.
By him who was in the living cloud babbling to the dark God,
a woman perfumed with the cat-heat of near-intelligibility.

Travel, says the book, to the dark root of the flame shaped world.
There, in central murk, I, Uncle, I, vocational, hierophantic adolescent,
nude in tongue as the prophet's volumes-speaking silent nakedness, wild,
there I, drawn up, kicking, drawn up with a curse, into the Vagueness
– blue as thunderhead, ripening like a grape – at the A-peak, the alpha-spot
of my eyes, there I, Uncle, draw breath,
surprised, there draw from groin-root the good breath.

Call To Worship In A Mass For The Life Of The World

Come you with desire and you without desire
          and you royal-sleek with the aplomb of the doctor-loved mad.
Come you who violently wait.
Come you brow bejewelled with the cranial ache to eat
               – bright, mental food – the world.
You sowing in tears, come.
Come you sleepless ones who hear in the clank-tappa-clang of unstable titanium heads
        banging walls of silos in wind-boistrous Dakota
                    spirit-rappings of your own garrulous deaths, come; come now.
Come all who are infatuated.
Come you who are Hamlet-spooked.
Let the jails empty
And let come diddlers, two-years-less-a-day sniffers
                              with drooling sleeves.
Come fathers whose shame hands have burnt on breasts of Oh-eyed daughters
               in houses mortgaged at twenty per cent.
Come. Let the electric locks release.

Come you dangerous ones who have seen all that is solid melt into air
Into the hearing of these extravagant promises.
Come from the doughnut stands, the Trail's End Taverns.
Come you Vespuccis of the Americas of the eye.
Come, come now here to the peacelands and their white peninsulas
                                             which are hands raised, pax.

You seldom Nathaniels with leaping tongues, come.
The night eats towards us, its boot full of blood.
Dead Alden, poet, come, come from the night, the dead cough of your laugh gruffing
as the large-animal-feeding sound of sea gnawing rock, your face of smoke,
your head blurred with Player's Fine Cut's broken gold rings, come.
Brother William, painter, ex-crazy Ukrainian, come, arrive shy, robed, with birds.
Come women with scars.
Come mumblers after quarters, with your newspaper shoe shuffles
from the high-heeled, well-healed, Dior-cheekboned streets.
Come from the Thrift Villa, Mister Donuts, sanatoria, buckets.
Come children from the video parlour, your hands agog
with the miracle of deke and thrust that outwhizzed the machine.
Come you who believe the golden M of the blood meat bar
is all that remains of metaphysics, gold standing ruin of M, and that what
lies behind the gold slag is nothing,
night-nothing, alive simply in its anarchically pure impulse
of its hate of you,
just night, glued one by the gore of insects exploded
on the flashing windshields of the traffic.
Come, turn and come; bolt from the loveless cars idling in the street,
doggying wearying tails of smoke.
Come you with child and you without child
And you whose children are your own nursed selves.
Come into the held breath of the mute God, who,
seeing you, covers his face in awe.

Elohim Mocks His Images For The Life Of The World

Do not cling to me. I hate your sacrifices, despise your festivals.
I turn embarrassed from your Helen Steiner Rice looks fattening
upon the ice cream scoop curves of holy art.
Pull down the Mediterranean pietas erotic to the sweet toothed sense.
Do not "like" me. I will not take your pain away.

Upwrap the beautiful mind bound white and young
for the arousal of the power fathers as it grows slender to the bone.
Unwrap the beautiful mind.
Retrieve all amputations.
Repent with erotic shouts thought of me, cloudland's geriatric,
his cranky beard and the body of a farm boy or narcissist that ripples
to the tip of a nixing fascist digit, more musclebound than a mushroom cloud.
Forget, too, the lamb-y, metaphor-male, the groinless, bourgeois Jesus,
with his Easter-egg, candy-store-window eyes
ogling the cruciform crosspiece of his eyebrows.
If you meet such a Christ on the way,
kill him.
Do you wish to love? Do you wish to love?
Leave love. Love nothing.
Life is dark; life is dark at the no-place
of the shocked heart cut two by the bone-handled, thrice-bladed Word.
Life

at the breakpoint between spirit and soul is dark.
It is the unseen continent, past the Europe-edge of like
that announces itself a hundred leagues out with the smell of cedars
and with giant floating beds of trillium and ragweed. It
is the vast green fragrance of nothing, meek darkness,
that maps itself in mind by the cry of imaginary animals
mating inland.

Unloop the crucifix from the neck; let the neck be a naked neck.
Eschew the new Plato-man tucking his shirt in with a stick.
Forget the ear-to-ear *mmmmmm hmmmm*,
the dream of total health, the dream of permanence.

Lover, meet me between the joint and the marrow.

A Necrology

Travelling Among The Energies Of The Dead

Father Lord Maximus, look up from the golden *Tome to Flavian,*
The Elvis sightings have begun.
Love us for them.
This is not the madness of theologians.
Wind pushes light through the black grasses.
Plates are brought in from the deck.
The last little slosh in the beer bottle is killed.
This is the orthodoxy of desire, practised now even as we veer toward sleep.

The television composes itself for hyperduliation
with the story of a gentle bear saving a family on their holidays
lost in the woods.
The sightings here, there.
The first time is in Kalamazoo.
He is seen buying a large quantity of batteries at a variety store.
He has shaved the sideburns and lost the weight.
He is dressed in a white jumpsuit and is wearing a motorcycle helmet.
He says nothing.
The lights in the grass make us want to sleep, Father.
They are the thunderous, streetlamp twinkle seen along the outskirts of eternity.
Sirens begin on the other side of town like blood clots moving slowly
toward the brain.
And clouds appear. Sleep fondles us. The bear has risen to sniff
the perplexity of the family.
Later, in the same place, he is seen leaving a Burger King. He is thinner yet.
He puts on a pair of dark glasses and disappears in a light blue car.
Father, Confessor, the venerable eros to fuse all things under the double will of Christ
Is passed down to us like a snap-shot of a relative we no longer recognize.
Thus we are driven among the *logoi* of the dead.
Darkness flickers.
This is how it happens.

Grass seduces light to be with it, thigh to thigh each day, while the tree lives
To make the man in the house near it touch its trunk,
And the stone flirts with the girl to balance the slender vase of her loneliness on it
And rest it there. The girl sits down, drawing into her mind
What she remembers of the program of the bear, the mom, the dad, the kids.
Just as we court the dead.
This is the path of the Kingdom.
The union of all things without violence.
Maximus, you have seen the migrating flocks of divine energies twitching in the glitter-tree
of the *Logos*.
You have seen the teeth-clenched individualities of all things surge up
Then return to earth in the gull glide of the divine mind.
So you will know.

What will he say? What will he say? Tell us there are alien graveyards
Covering half of Africa, of the long life that comes swallowing G-H3 vitamins?
Lectures on fibre, happiness through astrology, covering veins.
Sleep is the last rite we keep from the great ancestral tribal liturgies.
We perform it by rote, alone, and without joy.
Still, come in. It's late and time to come in. Finish your beer. Slide the glass doors
closed. It is cold. How the subdivision shimmers this late like a jewel-
embedded book. Hey, did you hear the one about the bear that loved the family
To distraction? So. Now. Well.
Maximus, all things are rushing together at such singing speeds
The air grows drowsy and even the cars seem heavier. Our bodies are thickly
Smudged with gravity. *Elvis, Elvis.*
The television is a thrill of alpha waves.
Strand upon strand combed out, combed out.
They are more beautiful than long blond hair on a thin, preoccupied woman.
We imagine ourselves naked, waves of this hair covering us with its sleep.
So this is how the story ended: the bear was given a medal
And learned to drive the family car.

And rode off.   The end.   We are tired.
Those clouds, there, in the night sky, where just enough light is
To make things interesting, don't they look like the pineapples and pomegranates
Carved with tassles, because in those days every corpse was an aristocrat, carved
Round the showcase windows of mare-drawn hearses at the turn of the century?
Yes, yes.   The dead's black food which they flaunted but did not eat. The garden.

"Some enchanted evening, you will see a stranger
You will see a stranger across a crowded room ..."
So we wait.
Cars go north along the Michigan peninsula in the night
almost "free from the bonds of gravity and its fantasies."
Our hearts are camouflaged with motion and we do not see them.
North of the sightings the cars pass a sign for the Five Hundred Pound Man-eating Clam.
One comically horror eye flickers from the shell mouth upon a cartoon big-game hunter.
As the human race once looked upon the world.
The highways are dark as bloodstreams, as a sleeper's breath going in and out.
Further north is another sign for The Call of the Wild,
One acre of ceramic deer and moose,
Dead-eyed, scattered among bored poplars, admission $3.50.
The noumenon with a bullet in its head, nature in a pan.
Father Maximus, we still see with the old, great desire, but it is weighted and rotted
with a darkness like the depression coming after too much sugar,
And so when we see, we see him, the King, the eye's guess at what it's like
to swallow a milkshake,
And we are tired.
When we see him again he will probably say to us, you look tired,
And ask us to lie down, with him.
So, Maximus, *ora pro nobis*.   And why not?
Our craving makes us shine more than seraphim.

Three Songs For Calling Ghosts

Ghost Song

Pretty soon ... next spring. – Wovoka, ghost Messiah

Buffalo under the earth raise up a hundred-mile-wide dance.
Blood ribbons from their noses.
Their humps are bright rattles of wounds.
Hairy feet rustle the dark's tall grasses; green dust rains endlessly.
The buffalo are under the earth, they are under the earth, a people.
They dream towards afternoons of sad rivers, the hill's flute lines;
Soft roots full of breath go out from their mouths
Into the mouths of the astounded dead.
The buffalo dance. They dance up the medicine of everything being alive.
They wear bright shirts that bleep like radio transmitters.
They dance, thunder on their backs, as the turtle carries the world.
Under the earth they move, the buffalo, hillocking, mounting one another,
deaf from the compulsive guns.

One third of a man's soul quivers into rock, another goes up
To meet lightning.
A third flies all night into the body of a woman.
The buffalo kick up in tall dark under sod; in their humps, thunder's
White roots.
Yes they carry wampum for the New Earth, tail sections of veering aircraft, Sitting Bull's
Trick pony, Custer's baby hair forked in a stick.
They have with them the dead, laugh tracks of broken situation comedies,
meadowlarks, doorless refrigerators
To build their careful villages in the Mountains.
The dead are jumpy.
Each death has its own body, given it by the Lord. This is a
killer horse from Alberta foothills.
The buffalo calm them, standing by one, silently, for decades.
They will come back.   Soon, all, in the spring.
Earth, the green sleep, will roar up a great wave of itself, sweet, glittering
With fossils and wild turnip, and eat the white cities.
Crazy Horse's bulletproof silence will kill-dance on the mounded banks.
They will come back the egoless herds and their Lakota.

Ghost Dance Song

The dead go south
Along summer stars
Shuffle-stepping, their red shirts flashing crosses, eagle-marks,
Cookfires behind them hauled between two poles pulled by dogs.
Light echoes off their Winchesters.
The dead go south from the green buttes,
Among large animals dazzle-painted with lightning streaks, hail spots,
Red-sky-theme-tunes from John Wayne Westerns,
Devils of eagles spouting and spiralling around them, the sage-rubbed dead.
Every seventh step they vanish
Into loud trances and dream of us.
When they are gone part of them lives in medicine stones
Behind their ears under long hair.
The dead go south.
They go to be sacredly lost, so the buffalo,
The muscle of the earth, will come to them
And teach them the dream-opera of the new shining world.
At night they roost in particular trees, like egrets,
Pulling their guns up after them on ropes.

Ahead, along the ghost-road, the Messiah's glimmering tents
In Time's badlands, fire circle of eternal
Forms – the spotted eagle feather, the buffalo's
Will, dark forces, electromagnetism and dream, all seated around one fire.
The green infinite. Birds boil overhead, a man hunts in the passionate
Distance. Father, let the dead and this world come back out of the West like missiles.
Look, Father, give us again our arrows.
The names of the Seventh Cavalry are written in gravity.
Let them go down in Hell's sweet mouth. With Long Hair and gold share trading. Let
them go down in the forgetting shadow. Let them go down in the engulfment.
Let them go.
The eagle shall sow with the grass, the gopher with the white tail.
Let the whole world of the dead – it is rising,
It is humming – come back.
We dance.
The dead ghost-shuffle along the stars.
They dream of us. We stiffen and see them.
We return from this with trinkets of meat from extinct herds in our fists.
Fathers, let the buffalo come back, the new world rippling from their shoulders
like a cape, stencilled with moons, falling
creeks, animals, stars, light
in avalanches, grass
grown up to the second joint above the hoof.

The Whole World Of The Dead Lights Down On the Plains

The buffalo come back, trotting, thunder skewered into their shoulder blades
By bone hooks,
Dragged on long rawhide cords, humps flashing fire,
Herding the dead *yip-hee-ya* up the White River coulee.
Welcome, Brothers.
General Miles, tell your valet, now, to shoot you.
They carry lightning on their bowstrings, stormhead kill-clubs;
A wind leaps from the dead like a shadow;
Knives jewel from it, it spins;
It blades up earth in building-high combers,
A black surf roller coasters across the prairies.
Barbed wire flings up strands to protect itself;
The Seventh Cavalry dismounts and fires into the falling world.

Because the buffalo have smoked a pipe with the dark.
Because rivers under rock have given a feather to the canyon wall.
Because the dead have traded ponies, sweetgrass for fresh bodies.
Earth will launch its arm and count coup on money.
It will break money's windpipe.
It will seduce money down its mouth and scourge it forty days
into one eagle *scree*-ing over a Black Hill's cutknife.

So now, then, let the still-hung-over machine gunner leave his heated Sibley
And walk the half mile over the dead's frozen ditch at Wounded Knee
Up the rise to his stork-like weapon cozy in its sand pillows
And let him bow before its barrel, head flopping between knees,
And kiss his ass good-bye.
Sky slams earth.
Buffalo rake thunder across ground
As a dancer bump-drags his thonged skull around the sun pole.
Their humps gunship fire.
Bone hooks leap in their backs, a thunder nation
                                                            a thunder nation
Women give tremolo.   It is coming.
Stones suddenly remember where the horn spoon lost decades ago at Wolf Creek camp is.
Shoes fly from horses.
Glory zooms onto the flats and lights
                                              on the phallus of the buck antelope deep in the bluffs.
Grass grows in an exhaling rush.
The dead, rainbows from left armpit to navel,
Come.
With them the ecstatic geometry in the 1958 Chev tail fin,
Walking in a sacred manner, a fall of crow feathers down its back.
On warclouds, descending, seven new campfires.
Medicine visions seize again bloodroot in the ditches and on hills.
A one hundred car ore freight from Bismark to Hermosa
Slingshots into air,
Becomes a goose V whip-cracking north into late snow rolling down from Grandmother's Land.

There, in the afternoon, lying on my side,
in my prison, a star churns over me,
not so big, red, blue, red.
Thick light untangles from my chest, blond thunder,
curling back into me from space.

Light is not like us.
It has no conscience.
It shimmies and jumps
or goes away.
It is naked.

Maria must hide pictures of the Passion
or I cry out.
A fever seizes me, I turn sick.
I wanted to see the small speck
that rode the nail into wood.
It contained, I believe, everything, shrunk down,
gardens, plans for cities,
the detail of a wing, carefully lettered in proofs.

In the forests of chaos, a silver-green deer moves.
Its name is symmetry.
In the rainforests of chaos, an oiled feather
curves back from the head of the doe-horse.
It is called love.

His neck and breast are a noon full of horns.
I stand up.
His fingers are deepening violins of an afternoon's sleep.
The light is good; it holds me.
It knows me more than I know it.
His pectorals shoot into the sky two gold puffs of helium.
Two tremendous eyes fill the host until
only the edges show.

After returning home from Assisi
my bones would not stop singing their tongues.
My limbs would soften though I stood so tense in my room
I made no shadow.
Perhaps I wanted to die.
Light separates in me
as cake in the glutton's mouth.
Tears wrench their anchors into my flesh
and I want just this, to be here.
Here, the fragrances of colours
on the mind's lit palate,
and voices go on in me
through the minutely growing night.

1

Everything has a soul.
A tree of metals, green, rises from earth, floating
                                        into the flower of the sun.
Here, a sign.   Coral-soul.   Mud-soul
        Stone-soul.   Everything desires, climbs,
forgets itself into yellow.
Gold's is ripest, asleep beatifically on the most arrogant branch.

2

I have kept my furnace raptured with the same white fire six weeks
        crying for secrets.
My garden glitters with handfuls of a spilt music.
Angel footprints, bright silt from flight.
Clues, clues.
Yesterday, toward vespers, starlings threw themselves across sky
        with such clear force, scattering and rebuilding, they nearly spelt out
          the verse in late Matthew where seven demons rip the Magdalene.
I saw that.
Write this down: earth pulls to itselfe love.
Starres cook out fever, aire wrinkles
    with this flux, then turns to salt. Then mud.
Ye earth.   Pouring down from starres.
My chymicals roast.   I have not seen my bed these four days.

3

The garden shakes and sways.
Trees near the laboratory rustle their occult names in the smoke,
Latin tags, letters in Aramaic.
Everything engines into the sun and gold.
Heaven decays whitely on the grass, green magnet
        dewed with power and idea.

4

I have seen it, the gold tree growing in the furnace glass,
and in the tree, the peacock spreading her tail.
Holy mercury, mother, sun-blood,
                        sperms in this gold's bloating trunk with a spiritual joy
                                                        pouring out a shining fruit.
Eirennaeus Philalethes, everything is the same thing.
Starlight rots into the world, air putrifies to flesh.
Gold is a child of heaven
                beneath archangels and human pain-cry
                        and can be got by a fermentation of skin.
I have not done it
but could.
All that glitters comes from death.
From death, ecstasy.

All Souls' Day

They do not love Death.
The dead sprint fists to hymn-frilly throats. Chaste, they are us-adoring.
They beefily snub His slinking lips, Death's Father Knows Best
twinkle, the sticky, theatre-grope, lastrow hands. The dead
shrug clear from Death's gigolo glib to be with us
as breeze fits the blind curve of a white hen egg.
Think of them, co-tribalists, off Vancouver Island,
fish-muscled, sleepsmooth, spines
flashes of operettas erupting through static, circling; their skin
is their bright will, a beaming glide that is their dream
their eros and emotion.
They rise and fall in groundwater's plump organ music.
The dead sigh back in plough waves from gull-cruised tractors.
Their staticky torsos surf in and out like Radio Moscow through the spruce
of Northern Saskatchewan.
The dead are more than the boy's blond, Hellenic eye exhaling forevers! physiques!
which voltage the world; with stones they sing the landmass real.
Their waterlogged palms are full-black with Beethovian sighs.

Hallow, hallow, hallow the dead; they jilt Death's sleek mouth,
His too-warm, mentholated loveroom.
They nuzzle and weedle; the dead crave to tell us "Death's
Victor Mature lips mean nothing."
They flirt among us on longlegged voices, singing soprano idealisms
that raise the hills.
Wasp-waisted, the dead, spirit's sweater girls. They love us. They glide about
on their ballroom voices.
I find them, eloquently pectoralled, among the corn's hagiographic gestures.
I love them with a shout and wake them. They dance with the world,
their partners are dream homes off Consolation Nook shimmering in vertical brain light,
those erosed upward Platonic fractions of an inch in love.
They love us.
The dead lingua franca stones' slow, ghostly Latin, stones' Benedictine hum.
The earth drifts softly together.
They do not love Death.
They love the stone hands deer-leaping from cenotaph to sword hilt.
And they prayer-doze in the song around hydro wires tumbleweeding up the Fraser Canyon,
and in the Black Hills, along outcrops, where stones push up like ruptured navels
and first snows lie down with the lion-coloured grass.

Hegel Sees Napoleon at Jena, 1806

Painted to his horse, the world soul.   Your testicles you inhale so hard they hang
just a little below your earlobes, primitive charms. Never
had you thought to see Spirit....
You wanted to paint breasts, quickly, Eskimo-style, to your jacket. There
                    was the voice of ancient male darkness in you
                    hernia-ed to objecthood, *adumbratio*, terrifying and erotic.
He is real and he does not know what he is doing.
Your head-blood cherokees a leaping scream, one eyelid falls.
Never had you thought to see Spirit
so lazy-eyed, so gaily off-duty in eccentric disguise,
hauling tobacco through a sulfurous shark's fin
nose, thickening
in his ballerina tights,
worse than world-sick at thirty-eight.
He is the dialectic itself hyperventilating with extra-marital sex and twenty hour days.
The dolphin shape of the emperor, girlish and of incalculable intelligence, rubs
your town between his forefinger and thumb.
He feels "astonishingly well."
Your gigantic libido falls out to him as a dog's tongue.
The magnificent confusion of his face over the wolverine jaw is a masterpiece
of incompletion you lust to fill with bright bits of yourself,
and love.

In The Earlier Lives of Crows

They visited the dead a couple of times a day.
When are you coming back, when are you coming back?   they'd ask.
There were plans.
The dead just then were monkeying with this gigantic wind.
It was fitted with a 442 mill from a high-school, mid-sixties Chev, its carburetor
        a converted Bill Haley dance croon, eight or nine football fields,
          apartment buildings high, transparent, white teeth
              at the top curling like surf.
The idea was for an invasion like a massive coronary,
the dead-carrying-wind chugging toward the planet like a fist.
The crows liked what they saw, loved it.
Hey, they said, what about the Indians coming back, sky thick
      with meadowlarks and miles of buffalo to eat in the long, green afternoons?
They brought the dead mirrors, coins, a remark
some talk show host made last week.
The dead would peer deeply into these
trying to see the full light of their faces.
Densities, densities.
Memory before the attack had to be lined up like star houses.
Who played the father in *My Three Sons*?
What was the taste of orange?
Nothing happened.   The wind rotted in a field of heaven
into an unoccupied, gold stare.
Celestial ages creaked by.
Endless arguments over the roster of the '64 Boston Bruins.

Crows now swim over the telephone wires near my mother's.
One has died and lies on the ground.
Its soul floats up and gets locked into the talk
drilling through the wires.
What did you say?   says the man at the other end.
What?   What?

More Beasts

Christmas Eve And The Bull

His bloodweight is nights of organ music in a big angel-breasted Italian cathedral,
rain clouds stumbling down the Andes;
he twists it in the socket of his pen,
will-steers his moonmachine girth, his inspired gravity to butterfly-touch
on his gold nose ring,
The theological shape that hypnotizes him, there, at his end,
where his great-as-libraries self-Summa must rest, syllogistically,
for order in the snow-amnesiaed fields and the barn to be.
His stare nails his head in one place; nine pound woodsplitting hammer back feet
diddle a twitchy rhumba before his tail.
The bull's teenage handsomeness swaggers along his curly breath.
O bull.
O he is huge in the barn, a Friday night T-bird radio turned loud, pontifex, muscle
of a falling wall,
Assyrian horn root bangs and his rubbery moo.
His nudity is a proof for God.
La-la. Tra-lala. Tiptop, topdrawer, the ticktock best bull is Elvis-dear, sacerdotal,
lost-glorious as the Bulgar throne's claimant, la-la!
Let the barn be his sensorium. Is. Each udder, silage fork is bull
in self-procession.
"Whan that Aprille with its showres soote," he lauds in his blood tubes.
Baba-boo. "Adeste fidelis"; his loins are operatic. His crown curls are the plump
frolic of ceiling putti.
Soon Christmas. His eyes let out their breath.
The bull's horn is flesh "humming" Vivaldi to itself.
He is God's dream of geometry fiddled to the power of the bone.
"I am God's erotic dream," the bull thinks.
The barn is weightless, floating on balloons of cows' breath.
"I will hold the bouquet of myself and smell deeply."
Minty one, hill of glories, hallow on hallows, shining
bull, hormone engine-roomed, courtier thighed, gimp chested
with Hank Williams' hurt,
He wolfs the heifers with his tattooed heart, and listens for snow.

Snow grinds itself in circles to darkness across the yard,
a battery slurring into its stump.
The farmer settles down, flu fumed in red socks, to watch television.
Let's Make A Deal; the host is dressed as Santa.
Snow grindspits from snow,
lathe-chips worried from the dark world.
His banker, twenty miles away, in town, now slides in his chair in the bright
subdivision; his food is dark and evil as Plotinus said it must be.
His meat does not sing or praise; nothing hears his knife flash; he pities
the meat's tin ear for abstraction as nineteenth century evangelists pitied Africa.
Snow steel-shavings from snow across the yard as darkness frays from a sleeping pill.
The tractor in the farmer's arm sleeps; his unshaved-as-a-pirate,
ploughblade jawed father is asleep on the horse blanket chair.
Neither worry. There is no worry.
Tomorrow the bull's nude gravitas easily will boost-start the morning stalls.
A calf spacewalks three aisles down, drifting round and round
in his mother's stomach blue-blank.
Ace of the World, Grace-Blood, follow him for joy; join the sleepy air.
But the bull will not move; he grips floor reverently in his shit toes.
Sky's no longer home.
Soon Christmas, soon the royal o'clock when metaphysics blew through flesh
And caught on a barb of bone.
He's for the kingdom of here, then.
The big girls sleep on their food, drugged in milk's soap opera plotlines
and dream, their Manichean black-white neither good nor evil, chained
as illustrated books.
Wood cracks under stars in the south woodlot.
The beams above him grope, man and wife, together, in the dark,
sighing out.

I Bow To It

Earth, earth, earth, stone lobed, blue, earnest,
blundering Godward with lummoxing barn fever, the dead's reliquary, the dead
bunched as flowers in its arms, the stone-sung-to
dead, the lovely, horse-sensed,
devout earth, jewelleried with the dead, earth,
earth, dog-adored, wise and ambitious sleep, anti-fire, intelligenced
with diva-fat, cadenced purpley as the long Book of Isaiah, the slow
exhalation of itself, earth, wasp-pasture, dragging a shadow
of water, singing trampoline of winds, moving, bee-brocaded bosom
first, bright in the dark ray of its tonnage, bright in the dark
ray of its tonnage, potato-ganglioned,
bright-dark, unfolding.

Part Of The Inheritance

For Susan Shantz (shrine-builder)

The hoards of sleep surround us.
Cast up, great mounds of it, termiteria,
chewed and hardened.
These are the very palaces we live in,
handed down through the family,
set on clipped parkland rolling away from the eye.
Parts of it are very old.
One passageway is weddingcaked
with heavy, round figures of an out-of-date joy.
It was begun with great ambition over a hundred years ago
in Northern Ireland.
Men in tight red hunt clothes
from the *Illustrated London News*.
It wanders off uncompletable into the dark.

In one of the rooms a collection of gadgets
for perpetual motion.
Sleep has projects that go on
even after the sleeper has died.
Go to the balcony and enjoy the lilacs'
mimesis of everything alive the day your parents got married
over fifty years ago
Now come back quickly from the window.
If you are seen in sleep by what is
outside in the night, it is not good.

When we drift off we go to become characters
in the long, untranslatable ancient sutras of the night.
To live here means one or two responsibilities
unspoken but known.
Keep them. Sleep is
the elder son who died
so you could have the inheritance.

Poplars know everything about sleep,
their glossolalia saying even more than the *New Catholic Encyclopedia*,
speaking sleep's endless hexameters as a child syllables til her mouth blurs,
so I'll ask them, rosarying there in the wind, Saskatoons ripe-dopey under them,
if they think there's a true world next to ours
that sleep, the animal, visits often because it feels more at home there.
And I'll ask them if they think this shadow-place, sleep's nook in the country,
is not a shadow place at all, but the place where the grass elopes to,
or water keeps its money,
or at least where those nostalgic shadows in long grass in July that make us
wish we were born grass come from.
I'll ask if this world which is not a shadow-place but seems to be perhaps isn't
the true, flat lap where we sit, asleep or awake, when we hear that well-known voice
rushing past us, pure force,
expertly thrown, that ventriloquizes our lives into place and some kind of order.
Ah, telos.
All the lovely darknesses in the world growing out from there.
Rain engorged over cut hay, bees fattening over roses.
Where the shadows of light are truth itself.
This is what I want to know. Is what we are really doing, *really* doing
with our lives whether we think of it or not,
a beast, or one of those forces that terrified Newton changed into an animal
galloping along in the dark afternoon of that other place, the one, lovely home
place, intuiting its way through the grassy savannahs they have there,
thinking out from between its shoulder blades?
If so, then we're completely at home in the real world.
All the lovely darknesses.
I have no doubt the poplars, masters and mandarins of sleep, could give them to us
chapter and verse, and tell us of all this together, the world, the whole
seen and unseen, how it's
ingeniously physical, and how it makes sense, not by doing anything, not by using
some bloody verb, but just by growing fatter each day with variety
as when magpies pass a song through the trees at 6:00 am like a basketball
at a Harlem Globetrotters warm-up,
until the world gets into that happy numb state where judgements become even more
gorgeously impossible and love gets fluid and doubletake-sleek
as showboat acts fluked off in dream.

Chant For The Feast Of St. Francis

I love the tree.
It is standing to speak in the fire of itself.
It is great choirs rising to sing
the tree's long quiet.
I love the grass for it is strong.
I love the stone. Its dark eye
leans against my breast-knuckle.
I love the stone, the stone's here-next-to-us;
the *seriousness* of it holding itself
                                        just where it is
floats the world.
I love the earth, to sleep luminous in her ear.
The dead are beautiful, they are horse-shy,
their manners shining like chandeliers on ocean liners.
When we sleep
they crane forward to touch us and read
to us from their book.
I love the nothing that blooms in the dark
brightly
and is our last food.
Breathe softly
through the groin. Touch the tree, show
your palm to the stone.   Kiss the stone.

Hawk

He takes
the Greatest Hits of Fabian,
Teilhard de Chardin's pensées,
and Bernini's Ecstasy of St. Teresa,
plots it all out aerodynamically
into kill-paths and exact head twists for sizing distances
and, like that, it's him gliding
over to me
barking in falsetto *Ya stupid shit* *Bozo* *Hike off*
He's done something brilliant
with the sky, correcting it into himself.
Ah, Concupiscence, I love the way your circling
holds murder at slow, steady boil.
Laughter, crying, shouting show out from his feathers.
The belly is calf-curve of a beauty pageant leg.
He turns his head in tight machinery jerks
to take in me beneath him.
He doesn't know me from St. Thomas' third proof
for the existence of God, a pound of hammers, from a night club
act paying tribute to Wayne Newton.
He doesn't believe the colour blue exists.
He hears the wind scrape over the Rocky Mountains
four hundred kilometers to the West.
He thinks the world is red like the small drop
of oil in his eye.
Linebacker-souled, Sharp-shinned or Cooper's,
he warlords the hot pine rows, eyeing
two and a half times more than what is there, spiffy
in his fastidious rage.

What keeps him over the trees half a day
fussing and rocking, nest or corpse, I haven't found yet.
Maybe he's just staked the plantation's northwest edge
as ego's homebase the way we'd draw a line in the playground dust
and say cross this and you're dead.
I want to take him on, hormone to hormone.
That's why I come out and stand inside the flexing circles.
Kreeee   Kreeeeeee   Kreeeeeee   I am rabbit-punched.
His open wings look like love itself.
Here is loving into the very center of the earth.
White, blond, black.

Satellites tip and yaw high overhead in a daylight
that makes them absent.
They are full of souvenirs of us, the loneliness
          of instruments, breath pauses in a countdown series, 1969.
Later I go to weekday Mass in the monastery chapel,
the room shadowy, dense,
and eat the host and suddenly
I'm what the hawk is.

St. Peter's Abbey, 1988

Spirit Of Agriculture, 1986

for Louisa

1

Barn light
great as gold room-sky at the Council of Trent
at the definition of papal infallibility, joy's fist-like body, then,
raised over the elegant *periti* like a stadium shout at a touchdown, light
pleased as a rich man's belly, gold heat
summery and wavy over the mirage lines of argument, tongue's bright shadow, what
of the cardinal's eminence the muddy eye cannot hold, morning light
in the towering barn, now,
when the forearms of the farm are sleeping, this light
the goats wear as the more public part of their bodies,
as we wear fierce manes of feeling, monstrances of what might be
fanatically bright hair when moved.

2

And the barn suddenly like a circus family
climbs up unto itself, web
to twine-loop, beam
to web, hay hook
Everested to nail, loin chandelier of the one lonesome buck waving like one hand
free, weightless
Leibnitzean worlds of self-hurrah, architectures
of it-couldn't-be-any-other-way, apt as a high ear of violins,
as gulls mount the cross valley hill like a god's thought climbing a girl's thigh.

3

You who are about to be hysterical, look
at the stone
that looks back at you like your father.

4

The farms are dying.
The farms scuff in their nervous straw, throwing links of their machinery, laneways
fluting, meaty, vegetable ears
fanning with terrified stupidity,
half men, one and half men, shocked by the dark ray of their deaths.
Pale land of sleep.
There is a rumour among the farms
there is a place in the West
they must go to die,
where all the Indians have gone, land of dreaming,
the bone gone dreaming in a grease swamp, go
lie down, laneway love-holding lane end in going,
the grave-hair-faced farmers asleep in the howdahs of tractors
on their backs, and in the mornings
before milking, I have seen them moving
to that place like hills
moving.

5

Light like a gold ear, like the plaque angels hold over the right shoulders of the dead
        in old prints, light, the pectoral of a Mediterranean boy stretched in the pull-back
of bow arm, the point
in Music for the Royal Fireworks where the expert kettle drummer starts to sway
in an electrocuted wave, striking the skin over and over crossed wrists, weeping,
                                        animus roaring, maybe
                tapping the rim with his forehead like a sped-up ether bird,
propellering his mallets, and the violinist walks back and forth
on his instrument like a man who's lost car keys, the king confused and about
to rise, light like that or the mouth-shape
                of someone saying "yes,"
light that is where the word goes that slips the tongue
    and waits, the light.

6

Now the land turns in its chemical sleep, corn
floating on lakes of nitrogen, and the almost-awake banker dreams in town
of a sistine, jet-fuel-bright sky, money's salmon run
up the head office cloud shaft of a Toronto ziggurat,
an Islamic heaven
where women flicker like trout in the dark
pool of the chief executive's eye.
        He sharks out in the gliding skin of his sleep
skin sidepanelled with 30,000 feet's victory-bright aluminium, his eye
            jumping ahead of him like an ecstatic's unconsciousness red red red.
He cleans the highway of farms hit crossing in the night.
Ingenious hunger making him everywhere, kill-thing, his will-to-power
mouth loosewide in the meathead leer of a Wagner opera.

7

You who are about to be giddy, Spiritus Vertiginous, look
at your hand, the palm, its wise face, the place
in you the sun rests, breathing
soft hub the hawk feels as the center hold of its wheel turn.
        Raise it. It is the tablet of writing powers and thrones hold over the right shoulders
                    of the dead.
Look: the one you hold is gathering words. Filling with light.

8

Dawn.
One goat leaps to a place in the air near the manure pile
as if an angel rushed through the room
of her brain and flung on a light and the goat flew
up, fleshless, into it, the light the colour of its corn-tan eye, instantly
gone seconds
until the spirit-line earth
wills into the goat, into the eye of the goat from the shadowed love eye of the stone
grew taut and sprung
her back.

She looks back with all
the forsythia, Handel trumpet goldness
of her queer eye out of her Kilroy-was-here face
                at the air her non-body was.   Huh.

Letters, Dreams

and the world, with all it craves for…
– I John 2: 16-17

It should be given to all of us to weep.
– Simeon the New Theologian

It's Like This

Niels Bohr hear me.
The petroleum breath of God no longer goldly upstrokes
my spine's plunger herding a yellow-red roar to my head, which I,
in turn, sire to others,
mating bull cloud of cognitive vehemence.
The opposite of one profound truth, Love,
is not another, but pneumonia weather's walk at 2:00 am to Tim Horton's
to worship sugar, path worn in the tooth.
I exist but am not actual.
I live in the fat-fold of God's emphysemic eye.

Gerard Manley Hopkins, you with a mouth like a brassière strap showing,
do not hate me.
Not with the Maginot Line of your moral headbone hate me.
You would not have done what I
did: given.
Take your eye out of my left shoulder.
Stop the tieing and untieing of your cassock sash, clipped huffing
through nostril, the metronome walk back and forth,
the lion sweep of your beautiful head.
I have gone into matter
and seen new tribes: teenagers and cars
beneath the bull-roarer of the city's spirit tongue.

Like the cows in Hegel's field
I darkened with the darkness of unintelligible things
in the Babylon of the born to shop
by the metal rivers where nothing divides.
The man downstairs is yelling legends to his child;
he has known his new, blue Chevrolet in another life.
Sing to us, said the Lords of matter, one of eros' songs.
They asked us, our oppressors, for joy,
where, as the crowds rushed into the Fairview Mall,
nature was being sucked into history.

Turn to the darkness, said a sleeper's book,
and ask what it wants.
I hear the castrati, Gregorian, QED, Vienna Boys' Choir, deranged Delphi
"fuck you" of matter.
Gerard Manley Hopkins do not hate me.
This is a new place
with the lingua of matter and matter's Columbus ambitions,
and war plans of matter and the love-looking of matter at matter's
own juvenile face.

Among the lawnchairs and chocolates, revolutionary light
jerks up like Ahab's calling arm.

Imitating The Dark

A man approaches Nijinsky in the asylum. Pliés.
No, he does not recognize the animal of this gesture, not this, ho, ho.
Too bright, too clenched-lit, like a chapter on sexual cleanliness for adolescent
boys read through teeth by a soprano Mother. He has enough of this already
from the doctors. Besides, no, God is cloud not flame. *There.*
Another stance, then. He's well if he believes in even one. So. Feet v-ed. Poses
offered like flowers. The man stands before him, a dancer.
But each one is misspelled, pronounced just slightly wrong as if read only in a book.
God thinks to me in red arches, one marble voice, rising, rising.
Dance this.
The locked-in air snaps with electricity, sparrows. Birds. Brides. Non, no,
no – I will not marry this dancing. Its cake-top beauty
would rot through my armbones.
Look, says Nijinsky, everything has whistling edges. Names, objects. Even the air
is a thickness of plummets glittering
as guns from a hideout. Death, for example, is close
enough to kiss your hand; touch its hump, throw it in the air, olé.
Look, in the crutches night gathers as a tree of storks. In the wheelchairs
she sits whining. I am its secret husband.
Well then, I have a stone I love. There on the dresser. Dance its memory. Even
making tea, imitate the dark.
Picture a Gospel of St. John written in bulging gold script on a Greek island late
in the fifth century. Well? It has shadows, shadows deep inside it. My biography.
Zat, zat, zat, feet here, there; they bloom and die, bloom and die. Pluck them
and rope them around my coffin.

1. July 31, Feast of St. Ignatius

Monty,
spare-tired with sugar of self-
love, a failed monk, I gross out now more than light.

My head rots
in a perfume's gold crust; there, hived in the aurantine smell,
I am disaster's party trick
and transubstantiate backwards, wax, prosper
into plurals of one,
am swollen as a kept royal egg. I am well, Monsignor, I am
rabidly beatific. But brain-fire gutters
to a cozy stump of flab.
I am eaten by my flesh.
It mounts me, manic and bug-eyed,
as a grain-toxic steer claws up its brother's back in July's spinning pen.

But, hey, good news: My tummy is sweet now
and smiles like a bishop over the lambs of my feet.
Diamond-neck, wear this close: I have been to hell.
There were acres of underground parking garage.
The cars were vacant-dark, windows scented with breath.
And here I found only Robert Lowell, phallocrat,
cruising the waiting slots of the puppy-love place, adoring
what grew and melted on the black windows, baboon-arse-red behind his exploding
cigarettes, clenched glasses canted badly,
infinitely himself,
car radio dialed to static. Happy?

Who here is not happy; all are happy as demoniacs.
After lust, Abelard loved death.
His mind grew into a necropolis, angels cute as cheerleaders.
My senses rush among the tombs, candy-bright, howling. The ego
studies its marble profile; the stone rivers to honey in love-light
and decapitates itself.
I have lost judgement.
You are my witness, frére,
my wits once were slender,
whaleboned by the Summa;
                    now I roll outside my underwear.

You say I hate the world.
Ha.
I do.
I hate the world, not just because
                    my girlfriend's toe nails are red,
but only to love it rightly in the best Presbyterian-cum-Plato way.
Listen, everything must heat into spirit.
Flesh must become feather and feather must be the sword to carve the body.
The world must be roaring, numinous, white.
                    I have always wanted to explode. There's
"ideological differences" for you!
I want to go up in peacockery of Plotinian flame.
Decayed now. I speak the worst.
                    floridly, hot as a sparrow,
                        the pseudo-Friedrich Nietzsche.

2. Reply To a Letter Dated August 21

"… so filled
with a dark Romanticism, its anger of the world and Word. I suppose
quick eros
for the Absolute destroys."

So, thus, I'll tell you; it was like this
an unSocratic denouement. Again and again
leaving.   Regina-reared on the beatitude of meat
and potato, I gourmanded
the cuspid-collapsing bonbons of elsewhere.
My heart's teeth wore black with sugar.

One had me Oldsmobiling with kinetic love's wealthy roll, carpeted
by the tops of eight round fires,
ubermensch's carbohydrates, eight
flathead-cylindering in a plenum of contiguous Saskatchewan nights,
                                                  deep in the dialectic,
more in sky than on earth, up,
north, towns, dogs thrown wrestling at the tires, gone,
past farm yard lights working an exact
gravity on the sparse, in-sleep-lighter-than-air Holsteins
          to keep them from boasting into space like individual St. Pauls,
car forearm and pectoral of my will, will crewcutted, American, jawed
                                             like the little red engine that thought it could,
            north,
through Melfort, Prince Albert,
last miles through sock burr and stubble to the first
awe-brained pines on foot, through snow crust, night slick with mink,
and there saw the sky like a woman removing her clothes.
There above the dark Germanic consciousness of treeline
the long-legged Northern Lights unloosening and moving
                              within her veils and red silks to my peep-show, rocking,
                                             thirteen year old eyes – and look
at me now,

look.   A ruin of angelism.
Thought's white tusk rolls on nerve-dead root, like a bored child
                                                swaying on its mother's shopping hand.
Metaphysics has hot-plated the brain to slop.
The world bulks to dark, to evil gravities.

Well, listen, so what if I'm fat-arsed Sittlekeit with jade flames
barking tiresomely out of his head.   You, you,
however, with your story of Yeats and the last-creatures-copulating-
in-foam poems, written after the Geneva implant of monkey balls,
and you, under the table at the hymn-chirping party, angling teeth
at the toes of passing women, you, your
half empty Scotch glass protruding like an organ
detached in a Russian experiment of the 1950s,
reciting, under the table, Whitman, *death*, *death*, etc.,
Love, in case you haven't read the omen, have, of course, sed contraed yourself.

Because I did not say "death."   This "death" out-bellows, beyond Siegfried's, goes
                        more Lord Byronly into the dark
                                                than the worst of my exploring nil.
I did not mean the "death" that Romaned off your tongue.

Besides, believe me, I pray still.   Couvade, I process to my hand-wringing sheets
Christmas-morning-boy believing I grease the inching birth, by ritual rest,
                                                            of the fresh ousia.

3. November 30: All Souls

Hope's arse bloats hemorrhoids big as sandbags. We sit.
How long, O Lord, how long?
Dutchies and Hawaiians bought at Tim Horton's near the closed Gulf
Station that is soft and round in its light as the soul
        of a dead child, wing-wrapped, in a Victorian print,
shovel fire into the eye furnaces
of people insane in the street.
Road salt has eaten their legs to the knee.   But to them the Eye Roarer
                                        within the sacramental donut
comes, to the loto-dreamers, necromancers of random numbers,
                                        lights on the toqued woman
who is the Death of Concupiscence seated at the counter,
friends, filling them with near-love.
They are hot, here before the white mirrors, breathers
a few, of glad lithiumed air, the dangerous in dream, some royal
or near, gore's living aristocrats posh on disability pensions.
The last evolution of Spirit.
The Roarer hysterics in them like a sword-shoed mahdi,
hectoring for purity, power, the flesh picnics of jihad from steeples of blood.
                                                        He hates
both capital and women.
                This is the condition of Platonism
                    among the lumpen, 1985.
I am there.   I am with them.

We each want to be light, the first body.
    Lead us, Lord, not into the Valley of the Shadow of Desire.
But attend to the chest-deep, curious,
eros-volted, forward-craning that is the titillation in the unadult hand
vandalling a grocery bag for the chocolate bar. Sure,
OK, a sparrow, yes.   I said that.   But only to fulfill the theatre
of defense, pivoting round the gimp of a not-really-broken wing.   A trick,
see?   All that Nietzsche, Abelard, Lowell shit – it was like a dog
offering another its neck: like me; I'm dead.   I unspeak that.

Speak that breakneck we dream careening
at terrifying speeds, perhaps nowhere.
The beauty-marked German shepherd with a face like Voltaire, night dog
at the Rent-A-Wreck garage, with enough of the afternoon off to look my way
                    a full minute when I go in to visit the coffee machine,
holds me in contempt.
He loves the world.
We, he notices, ache for heaven.

4. Late Winter, 1986: Last Letters, Queries: What The Hell Is Happening?

"This is amazing. This is also bad. To bruise the body to pleasure
soul. Like coincidences with evil
something gets killed and does not recover in that path. Maybe God
is tricking you into the wilderness
to clean up your heart, whatever.
Anyway, anyway. When you write
'I need to interpret you like a hieroglyph,'
does that mean soon, care of the doctors, the struggle will
cease? One last word: Good hunting."

Amen, amen, good hunting.

Well, our talk, brother,
this archness, this hernia of tongue, brain's meconium:
We lawyer back and forth a mouth-prose of Gregorian bar talk,
us, that makes one yearn for an ear
on the swaying wire of water carrying the easy
voices of whales at party-line gossip.
Matter utters unto matter over the back fences of form.
Let *us*, however, be naked, clear.
I am glad, Your Grace, then, of the Incarnation, and love it.
What else is there to say: just that the failure mirabilis of Abelard's brain
                                        (back on this, I'm afraid)
perdures in the noosphere like a warm pee-spot in a Saskatchewan lake, lo,
and sad on him, the walker, sad on him whose thigh is rubbed
                                        slack by that feline heat.
For blood, I warn, will habit him to the place,
          and his chromosomes will rot and will mimic the creamy decay
            of that August place and he will fall in love with himself there, and there will be
                 no going. I fear that.
It is a dark time.
The heart leans forty-five degrees out over its shoes
like Nietzsche and Paul Reé in the picture of them pigeon-toeing
a whip-toggling Lou Andreas Salome in her two wheel wood cart mere inches through
impossible mud. Each joggle of her whip, the lives of the men leap
forward, jerking in sleep, and they are re-born second, third and fourth times.
Queer the heart that is Ben-Hured by a half-dead woman,
                 who wants, who wants, who wants. Lou is laughing.
Is she the Christ
or shall we wait for another?

Finding The Horses,
Dream At The Turning Of The Year, 1985

The pinto and chestnut quarter horse are lost in the city. Light driven
from sky. I know them both from the Guelph farm, the chestnut has legs like a
woman's. O the city is dark with hammers, tools' spiritual lives. The police
search house-to-house, waving, rolling their ox shoulders. They turn up the horses
in the three square yards of garden behind a Toronto semi-detached, black-purple
air squeezing in around them. I have been sent here to this neighbourhood
to keep the life of a good monk. The horses are spooked by the police
and kick-leap a couple of fences into a neighbour's yard.
The man whose yard the horses land in doesn't like what's going on.
They're throwing off my reception he yells.
The horses are sweating out great, white ghosts in his yard.
I've been away buying groceries, bright food, visiting a new grocery store
in the area, admiring it with my mother. I get back. I have lost the right to be
told the horses are here, they are injured. I go next door with just
my bare hands.
The man doesn't want to let me in, too many people in his house, his garden boiling
whiteness, there's a shining froth of will twitching over his head. But his
wife shouts at him I know the horses. OK he says. Do something about it.
I go out, find Babe with a piece of wire stamped through her nose; twisted in;
a sloppy dangle of wire is torqued 108 times round her neck, tight;
red, white lawnchairs are caught, battering, in a great loop of tangled, floating
wire she drags behind her. Here is my interior life. She's down,
thrashings have knifed up the grass. The wire comes out, curling little shavings of smoke.
Come on, I say, Love, come on. The dreamless life is a sinful one.
The man's t.v. lights up with secret Talmudic messages as we pass.
The night in its last blocks and crescents
turns slowly on itself, dense, granular,
scraping to exhaust all its oil of breath.

Grace

Headlong on the Parkway, the cars almost touching at 100 kph, his engine bellowing,
his head the faintest, arrowing tip of his mirror-smashing, out-of-orbit, beyond-
returning heart, the shot-past-forty Franciscan, hurtling at the lip of his calling,
in a borrowed Lincoln, accelerating for a white-knuckled appointment with his
august, marble-eyed psychiatrist, who tells him *now now*,
remembers suddenly swiiiii
iiiiiingngngng into the passing lane, the chassis rocking
on its frame, the gutteral, multi-syllable, sprung-rhythm Marghi word
for absolute happiness
taught him ten years ago in the mud bar of the Horizontal Hotel in Nigeria near
the Atlantika mountains by a drunk peanut farmer.
Not the word itself
but the existence of the word.

A hawk is motionless over a field of goldenrod, paintbrush
ten yards across the shark rush of traffic. He sees it. The hawk glitters
like the numinous word whose existence he has just recalled
and treads air in his humming head with the quivering word.
He sees it and thinks at heart dead-drop speed, for no steady
reason
of John Berryman
nicotine-knuckled poet, commissioned to sell encyclopedias
in Harlem, door to door, after the Depression and selling
none and the dark rising in his brain, menacing
his sigh-white, cry-peaked face, but not
the bird-shapes of words, them undrowned, undead
floating
over Berryman's mental Atlantis, where not even mountain
tops or Manhattan's cement Matterhorns peeped.
He thinks of Berryman, the poet. Of the still hawk.
And of the surely flimsy world honeycombed with the gaping mouths of the omnipresent sick;
thinks of the highspeed, metallic twitch of the city that jerks nervous around him,
a St. Vitus dance of matter, and of the delicate creatures, their hands exposed
to their wrists, hovering bent at the bucking controls;
thinks of the pale, holding-on young men standing at traffic lights,
their vertebrae wobbling like plates spun on a stick, frozen as children about to be
taught to waltz, and thinks of the women standing in front of kitchen mirrors,
Chopin on a tape, peeling apples with juice-weeping, shaking, gasp-long, noon-sharp knives.

The 100 kph Franciscan carries in the speeding tip of his forehead, manned nosecone,
a paradigm, pain bright.
It glistens like the word and the hawk.   He thinks of it
as part stone, callus-yellow, goose-egging his soul's rubbed tip,
                    jewel in a frog's forehead; thinks of it, too, as the broken end
of existential perfection, a cranial glitter half eaten by dark
                              the half he carries of the light that is the Life of the World,
the half he must mate, at great speed, quickly, before he gets too old
and doesn't care, lock, join, *coitus intellectus*, with its must-exist, bright Other
                                                                                    (word,
                                                                      or bird, or bright
                                                                         perfect spiritual glint)
like two halves of a torn dollar bill carried by rendezvousing spies into a dark country.

Thinks, too, of the hawk, now past, quivering in the rear view mirror, grey mark
of the still air, bobbing in the traffic's wind,
over the shoulder's permanently-pressed-north sow thistle, floating, the hawk,
over the earth, like a Berkeleian mind above a body its hunger has invented;
thinks of this hawk, wing-word,
                              hovering mind above the life-bright jewel of an invented earth,
and is aware of the absolute necessity of the presence of grace.
And therefore its presence.